Ancestors Said

Ancestors Said

365 INTROSPECTIONS FOR EMOTIONAL HEALING

Ehime Ora

HAY HOUSE, INC.

Carlsbad, California • New York City
London • Sydney • New Delhi

Published in the United States by: Hay House, Inc.: www.hayhouse.com®
Published in Australia by: Hay House Australia Pty. Ltd.: www.hayhouse.com.au
Published in the United Kingdom by: Hay House UK, Ltd.: www.hayhouse.co.uk
Published in India by: Hay House Publishers India: www.hayhouse.co.in

Cover design: Leah Jacobs-Gordon
Interior design and composition: Greg Johnson, Textbook Perfect

Cataloging-in-Publication Data is on file at the Library of Congress

Trade paper ISBN: 978-1-4019-7475-6
E-book ISBN: 978-1-4019-7476-3
Audiobook ISBN: 978-1-4019-7477-0

10 9 8 7 6 5 4 3 2 1

1st edition, July 2023

Printed in the United States of America

For my family on Earth and in heaven.

Introduction

Do you remember your ancestors? They remember you. Our ancestral lineage extends all the way back to the beginning of time and stardust. The ancestral lineage is a direct bridge to the Creator and Source. When we remember our ancestors, we become cognizant of the holy divinity that lives within our own lives.

Many global cultures have long-standing traditions of ancestral veneration, in which the spirit of deceased loved ones is honored and respected. When we acknowledge, uplift, and remember our ancestors through intentional acts of veneration, we receive their assistance and cover ourselves with great protection. The ancestors also provide us with valuable guidance, which serves as a navigation tool through life's uncertainty and challenges. In the broader sense, connecting with our ancestors creates streamlined progress in our lives.

Our ancestors shield us from the wickedness of this world and bless us with prosperity that is unlike anything we've ever seen. When we remember our ancestors, we're able to thoroughly connect with the legacy of our family and community. Most importantly, we remember ourselves. Beautiful things occur when you finally come to realize who you really are—the ancestors' child.

We are not connecting with our ancestors—we are *re*connecting with them. When we engage in veneration practices for our lineage, we are reinforcing our center and foundation. For many cultures, the altar space serves as an incredible meeting place between people and spirit. The altar may be adorned in decorations unique to that cultural practice. It is a defining space for offerings, ritual, and formal communication with one's ancestral lineage.

Though the altar holds importance, it's important to note that there are other ways that are equally as valuable to venerate your ancestral lineage outside of a formal altar. The body is the bridge between the divine and the physical world around you. When you're taking care of your emotional well-being and physical body, you are honoring the lineage that shares space within you, in addition to making you more open to the divine guidance that your people have to share.

Place a hand over your heart and take a deep breath. Your heartbeat is a symbol of a particular spirit that refused to die out. Here in this body, your ancestors experience life through your eyes. In exchange for this, you carry generations of ancestral wisdom within you that extend all the way to the start of creation. You are the living embodiment of your ancestors—wherever you go, they will always follow. You have the ability to tap into this internal connection at any time through bodily awareness. If you're mindful enough, you'll be able to hear them through your chest—showcasing worlds of knowledge that you can dive into.

Even if you don't wish to see ancestral veneration as a spiritual practice, consider it to be moments of gratitude that you extend for being alive and acknowledging those who came before you with respect and adoration. Your existence is not by coincidence; it is by calculated orchestration. This is why *Ances-*

tors Said was created. It intends to nudge you closer to mindfulness through short prose and affirmations. When we offer some time in our day to journal, meditate, and realign ourselves, we create stronger roots and a clearer mind to connect with our ancestral lineage.

Ancestors Said is also a beginning point on your journey of generational healing, the process of addressing and repairing the emotional and psychological wounds that are passed down from one generation to the next. This type of healing is based on the idea that the experiences and traumas of one's ancestors can have a lasting impact on future generations, and that these experiences and traumas can manifest in a variety of ways.

The concept of generational healing has its roots in various spiritual and cultural traditions, including indigenous and African spiritual practices. In these traditions, an individual's health and well-being are seen as interconnected with the well-being of the ancestors and of future generations. Sometimes our particular triggers are not our own; rather, they are characteristics we have inherited from our family and ancestral lineage. When we analyze repetitive patterns and trauma that have a personal effect on us, we free ourselves from heavy generational weight. We also create space for future descendants to flourish without experiencing the shackles of the past.

It all starts here, with conscious introspection.

The meditations in *Ancestors Said* serve as excellent journal prompts that provide a great way to practice awareness and self-reflection through the power of the written word. Journaling is an incredible way to unwrap yourself from any mental webs and, in turn, it fuels your self-expression. Through writing, you are safe in the quiet presence of your ancestors as they gently encourage you to surrender. The reason why journaling brings immeasurable healing is the lack of pressure you experience as you write. Between the pages you are safe to go as deep as you'd like; when you feel like you've gone too far, you can always resurface above the ink to safety.

Ancestors Said is a call to action for the complete return of the self. Utilize *Ancestors Said* as prompts to engage in healing circles that address personal experiences. Allow the book to spark intergenerational dialogue and communication to better understand the experiences and perspectives of elders in your life. Bring the book with you on your spiritual quests, to family gatherings, workshops, events, to your community, and anywhere that promotes healing. You can even use the words in this book for personal rituals such as prayer, meditation, and ceremonies with your ancestors. Divine with *Ancestors Said*! Ask your ancestors a question and then open to a random page in the book. Trust that the ancestors will guide you to the page that contains the answer you seek.

Welcome to a yearlong spiritual journey. Invite your ancestors to accompany you on this path.

You are never alone.

January

1

JANUARY

This year you will stand up for yourself.
Do not cower in the face of conflict.
Even if your voice shakes and cracks,
do not give away your power.

Your destiny has never been to be passive.

2

JANUARY

Today has an incredible chance
of being filled with bliss.
A much-needed exhale will wash over you
as contentment trickles down your spine.
This newfound peace is not something
you had to earn, but something
you were already deserving of.

3

JANUARY

Affirm:

I forgive myself for all the times
when I denied my own love.

4

JANUARY

Doing your best is always better than staying still,
waiting with crossed arms for perfection to arrive.
What's within your capacity is already enough.
Sometimes the sweetest perfection lies within
simplicity and ease.

5

JANUARY

Your ancestors do not give you
slow times to punish you.
If you're constantly on the go,
when will you have the time
to reflect, recharge, and restart?
Stop trying to accelerate everything in your life.
Let things be.

6

JANUARY

A love that's larger than life is the only thing that
will resonate with someone who's out of this world.
A heart filled to the brim with stardust
and auroras must be handled by cosmic hands.

Someone so large who will not cower
from your height.
A person with their own orbit—an equal.
That's what you deserve.

7

JANUARY

May your ancestors give you something
to smile about today.

8

JANUARY

You have no idea
just how good life is going to be for you.
Wait and see.

9

JANUARY

Why do you want to be liked by people
who don't even like themselves?

Investigate this and finally free yourself.

10

JANUARY

You gotta resurrect the deep pain within you
and give it a place to live
that's not within your body.
Let it live in art.
Let it live in writing.
Let it live in music.
Let it be devoured
by building brighter connections.
Your body is not a coffin for pain to be buried in.
Put it somewhere else.

11

JANUARY

When we let go, it means experiencing
a different type of death.

It's okay to mourn all the things you thought
you'd hold on to forever.

12

JANUARY

Save some of your love for yourself too.

13

JANUARY

You don't need to be completely healed
to be worthy of love.
There is no checkpoint in healing
that makes someone more worthy to receive love
than someone else.

You are worthy of love.
Right now, as you are.

14

JANUARY

And when fulfilling love arrives,
may you feel worthy enough to let it in.

15

JANUARY

Before you pray for anything,
make sure you pray for a long life and good health
to see all your blessings through.

16

JANUARY

You don't need to jam all your goals
into January.
You have 11 more months.
Take it slowly and mind your breath.

17

JANUARY

The peace you're looking for
does not exist in the future.
It can't be found outside of you either.
Learn to live in your body while you're
experiencing the present moment.
This way, contentment won't feel so foreign.

18

JANUARY

You get to choose who to keep around you.
You are in charge of your own peace.

Choose well.

19

JANUARY

Affirm:

I am enough because I said so.

20

JANUARY

Your ancestors will greatly repay you
every time you choose yourself.

21

JANUARY

Sometimes beautiful things are owed to you.

It's okay to celebrate their arrival
and enjoy them.

22

JANUARY

Affirm:

Wealth flows to me with ease because
I am already wealthy.

23

JANUARY

You won't be able to get out of a tiring situation
if you try to destroy yourself on the way there. Putting unrealistic pressure on yourself
will not make you materialize your goals any faster.

Remember your gentleness and persist, slowly.

24

JANUARY

Your ancestors are smarter than you.

Those delays that are stopping you from progressing
further could be protecting you from so much.

Sometimes the obstacle is the blessing
that's being given to you.

25

JANUARY

There are days for work
and there are days for rest.
Today is a day for rest.
So, rest.

26

JANUARY

When your ancestors say
it's time for you to rise,
you will rise.
There is no deadline for success.

27

JANUARY

May you receive long-term blessings.

28

JANUARY

You hold a lot of pain from people
who will never apologize.
One day you'll be able to release the sorrow
from your bones forever.

29

JANUARY

Affirm:

I forgive myself for enduring cruelty in love
just because I didn't want to be alone.

30

JANUARY

Today feels like ease.
You are being given a chance to start over.

Welcome to your new life.

31

JANUARY

Take some time for silence.

There's a message that your ancestors
want to give you,
and it can't manifest in chaos.

February

1

FEBRUARY

You become your own enemy
when you abandon yourself for others.
Respect yourself.

2

FEBRUARY

If you're truly at peace with yourself,
it'll be hard for you to feel threatened
by others' success.

If you're content with yourself and what you offer,
and know there will always be enough,
you'll be able to create long-lasting relationships
that aren't threatened by jealousy.

3
FEBRUARY

It takes a lot of courage to be who you are.
May you never wish to be anyone else.

4

FEBRUARY

Respect your passion.
For it shows you when something
is worth fighting for.

5

FEBRUARY

Affirm:

I forgive myself for all the times
I abandoned my spirit just because
I desired love from an unhealthy source.

6

FEBRUARY

Choose to no longer feel guilty
for loving with an open heart.
You had no idea that your love
wouldn't be cherished in their hands.

Forgive yourself for not knowing
and choose to love once more.

7

FEBRUARY

You will soon see why the ancestors
had you wait.
You'll be glad you did.

8

FEBRUARY

Affirm:

I am deserving of all the blessings
that are currently making their way toward me.

9

FEBRUARY

You can give up for today;
just make sure you try again tomorrow.

10

FEBRUARY

It's okay to be alone.
You are worthy of your own time.

11

FEBRUARY

If you force things,
you won't see any progress in your situations.
This is a reminder to flow,
even during these moments of tension.

12

FEBRUARY

I pray that today you'll learn to feel comfortable
in periods of waiting.

13

FEBRUARY

Take some time for quiet today.
The answer to your question
will arrive in stillness.

14

FEBRUARY

Your heart is counting on you to take
good care of it from this moment forward.

Never stray too far from love.

15

FEBRUARY

We choose a lot of things out of loneliness.
Don't let love be one of them.

16

FEBRUARY

This year you should be like honey
and go where the sweetness is.
For you already know what bitterness tastes like.

17

FEBRUARY

We all hold dualism inside of us
based on the perspective of others.

Acknowledge the various roles you play
in different experiences, and be okay with them.

18

FEBRUARY

There are people searching for a type of healing
that only you can provide.
Through your art, through your music,
through your creations.

This is why you must believe in yourself.

19

FEBRUARY

True oneness with your ancestors leads to the understanding of the importance of community.

Destroy hyper-independence.
You don't need to heal by yourself.

20

FEBRUARY

As things leave your life,
it's okay to grieve over their departure.

21

FEBRUARY

It's okay to take care of each other.
Be kind to others
and allow them to be kind to you.

22

FEBRUARY

Affirm:

I forgive myself for thinking that I needed
to become someone else in order to be loved.

23

FEBRUARY

Clothes are another way that we can express
the colors of our spirit.

It's time to wear what makes you feel good.
So that way, your external world can feel good too.

24

FEBRUARY

The next love is going to be unlike
anything you have experienced.
Don't let the past make you turn down
something that could be long-lasting.

These new people entering your life
had nothing to do with your old hurt.
Open up.

25

FEBRUARY

Be loved by others who are not
ashamed of loving.

May you be directed away from those
who make it feel like it's an inconvenience
to love or be loved.

26

FEBRUARY

I pray that you shake hands with the right people
who bless you with what you're looking for.

27

FEBRUARY

Affirm:

I am enough. And I have enough.

28

FEBRUARY

We go after unavailable people
because we are used to the same old story
that we need to work hard for love.

29

FEBRUARY

The goal is to live very well,
so we can die at peace.
To reach the end so weightless,
so light, and satisfied
that it reaches our spirit.

March

1

MARCH

This month you'll learn how to
fully step into yourself.
Lean into the weight of your destiny.

2

MARCH

Trusting your intuition means you must stop constantly looking for validation elsewhere to check if it's correct.

3

MARCH

Affirm:

I forgive myself for believing
that I did not deserve true love.

4

MARCH

If you don't have patience with the people you love,
yet you expect them to be patient with you,
there will always be an imbalance.

Being too self-centered will create lopsided
reciprocity in your connections.

And those types of connections struggle
to survive the test of time.
Be mindful.

5

MARCH

Affirm:

I forgive myself for searching for love
when I have been right here this entire time.

6
MARCH

Place your hand over your heart
and take a deep breath.
What do you need?
Give yourself that today.

7

MARCH

Learn to let things be.
Sometimes you destroy more
when you decide to control.

8

MARCH

It's okay to miss them.
You are still human.
Instead of guilting yourself
for your humanness, reflect.
Your feelings need your attention,
and they can become a catalyst
for great healing if you allow them.
Process.
Take your time.

9

MARCH

Healing is simultaneously a labor of love
and heartbreak.

You will experience pain while healing.
Know that this discomfort is only temporary.

10
MARCH

Affirm:

I choose to focus on love
that I don't have to question.

11

MARCH

When someone lets you love them,
you must allow them to love you back.
Give and receive.

This is called balance.

12

MARCH

Pay attention to how your body feels.

Stretch more often.

13

MARCH

Love is not something that happens to you;
it is something you already are.
You are love.

14
MARCH

The reason why feelings are hard to let go of
is because of the memories attached to them.

To heal, you must feel deeply.
You must honor the memories instead of
trying to convince yourself they never happened.

15

MARCH

Let them go, with love.
This way, love will find you right back.

16

MARCH

Envision a beautiful life for yourself.
Speak the details over yourself each morning
and before you go to sleep.
Affirming abundance in your life
takes you closer to experiencing it each day.

17
MARCH

Be mindful of escaping into someone else or an unproductive habit when the healing gets difficult.

You deserve your own love.

18

MARCH

Even when you rest,
you deserve to be blessed.

19

MARCH

Affirm:

I forgive myself for viewing someone's
lack of reciprocation as a challenge
to convince them of my worth.

I forgive myself for looking for the places
where I wasn't loved, instead of being at home
where I was.

20
MARCH

You gotta start loving yourself
like you actually mean it.

Show yourself that you're not just saying that.

21

MARCH

You are not finding yourself;
you are just returning home.

22

MARCH

The next step is to simply wait.
But do not wait in fear.

Wait with peace,
because great things are coming.
Soon.

23

MARCH

If you're feeling stuck, speak to the heavens.
A path to freedom will open up.

24
MARCH

Pictures will provide you with more memories
to keep as you grow into yourself.

Capture your transformations more often.

25

MARCH

You don't need to only survive—you can thrive.
You deserve a luxurious life.

When you allow life to give you luxury,
you open the space for the ancestors
who were unable to experience it for themselves.

26
MARCH

Your ancestors look down on you with a smile,
because you live.

Simply enjoying your life is productive.

27

MARCH

Ask for what you really want,
not what you think you should have.

Look inside.
When you speak with authenticity,
you'll unlock greater blessings.

28

MARCH

All you need to do
is see your desires in your mind's eye.
Once you can clearly see and then feel them,
with all your being,
you'll be able to receive anything
in this universe with ease.

29

MARCH

Sometimes the blessings you get
are only for you to enjoy.
Not everyone needs to know what you have
or what you will get in your life.

30
MARCH

Your ancestors experience life through your eyes.
Living your life as full as you can nourishes them.
You being alive is enough for them.

On this day, let's recognize that being here
at this moment and doing our best
strengthens and fortifies our own lineage.

31

MARCH

Let love work itself out.
There's nothing you need to do but receive.

April

1

APRIL

You don't need to show the world
everything you love or share in it.
You can love these things quietly.
You can enjoy them all by yourself.

2

APRIL

Love and suffering cannot coexist.
Healthy love is true love.

3
APRIL

May you never be suspicious
of honest love.

4

APRIL

When you go through a betrayal with a friend,
it can be so traumatic that it changes the entire way
you perceive trust and loyalty.

Take care to protect yourself,
but don't keep your heart closed off forever.

5

APRIL

For this month, hoping is not enough.
You must know and believe.
Faith must reside comfortably in your bones.
Choose trust.

6

APRIL

Please follow your purpose.
Even if the journey is difficult,
even if you encounter hardship.
Because your ancestors have given you
this destiny for a reason.

7

APRIL

Pain can live in your clothes.
It can keep you stuck in it.
Be mindful to not stay in that place.
Open yourself up to light.

8

APRIL

You can be everything.
Your destiny is to be limitless.
Don't limit yourself.

9

APRIL

Boundaries are in your body.
Advocate for yourself
when you feel uncomfortable.
You have the right to be protective
over yourself.

10

APRIL

If you allow others to continuously
push you into rage,
you will know no peace.
Your anger is a precious energy source.
Stay wise.

11

APRIL

Others can try to emulate you,
but the blessings arriving have your name on them.
Others may try to replicate your process,
but they will never quite have the same success.

Why?
Because the universe is not a fool.

12

APRIL

Do not fall victim to self-imposed loneliness
by believing you don't need friends.

You deserve a community that pours into you,
just as you pour right back.

13
APRIL

Affirm:

I deserve to be this in love with myself
all the time.

14
APRIL

No one is paying you to hate yourself.
You'll be wealthier by having self-acceptance.

15

APRIL

It's time to start looking your best,
from your skin to your clothes.
Embody your own personal definition of beauty—
not anyone else's.

Allow yourself to be as beautiful
as your ancestors see that you are.

16

APRIL

You can only be taken off your throne
if you allow them to knock you down.
So, don't allow them.

17

APRIL

Was there a hobby or activity
you loved as a child?
Pick it up again.
Embrace childlike joy.
It'll make you feel alive again.

18

APRIL

Meet your ancestors halfway
when it comes to your aspirations.
All you need to do is try
and they'll take care of the rest.

19

APRIL

There are people in your life who love you,
honestly and deeply.
Do not let the betrayals you have experienced
keep you from them.

20
APRIL

No one is rushing you;
you are the only one rushing yourself.
Be mindful of creating so much pressure
on yourself that you break.

21

APRIL

Friends don't put each other on pedestals.
Create a mutual culture of respect instead.

22

APRIL

Let's start this day by choosing less suffering.
You don't need to suffer to receive love
or to achieve your dreams.
Let's choose ease.

23

APRIL

Kindness is good.

Kindness is something that you should never abandon or feel guilty for having.

The goal is to be mindful of when your kindness is being used against you.

24
APRIL

As soon as you realize that you cannot do
someone's healing for them,
you will start to take things less personally.
Do what you can.
That is enough.

25

APRIL

Invest in discernment when considering
the things and people you devote time to.
This investment will pay off.

26

APRIL

You're not as alone as you think you are.
Let your ancestors take some of the weight off.

Cry and break with pride.
Trust and know
that they will put you back together.

27

APRIL

Be mindful of venturing on this healing journey
with the goal to fix yourself.

You are not broken;
there is nothing wrong with you.
Healing is not to fix or erase
but to bring inner harmony with all parts
of yourself so they can properly coexist.

28

APRIL

Ignoring your purpose
will only get more difficult.
It's time to lean into it,
no matter how afraid you may feel.

29

APRIL

You are the only person
capable of fulfilling your dreams.
This is called destiny.

If it's not you, then who?
Still you.

30

APRIL

Each connection has its own organic destiny.

Release the need to make the temporary permanent
and the permanent temporary.

May

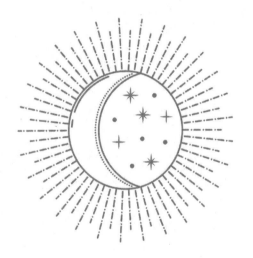

1

MAY

The caterpillar can only form its chrysalis
when it stays still.
The butterfly is only born after slow moments.
Feeling stuck or stagnant can be the precursor
for incredible change.

2

MAY

You will never have to convince love to stay.
You never have to seduce love to enter your home.
It already knows your address.

3
MAY

Unconditional love is the great healer of all wounds.
May you learn to extend this love
to your past and present without shame.

4

MAY

If you want to start aligning yourself
with greater love,
start rejecting the offers of love
that do not make you feel full.

5

MAY

The heavy energy is clearing.
Today feels like hope.

6

MAY

In this next chapter of your life, be more curious.
Give yourself more time for self-exploration.
You'll be surprised by the many talents within you
if you give yourself the permission to be a beginner.

7

MAY

Today may be filled with tidal waves
of new information and emotion.
Ride them smoothly and let yourself experience
the ride fully, without judgment.

8
MAY

Those old habits of yours won't work
where you're trying to go.
It's time to upgrade.

9

MAY

Suffering is not your destiny.
Ease is.

10
MAY

Allow yourself to exist
in any emotional state with peace.
Accept yourself in your happiness
and through your sadness with peace and love.

11
MAY

Your ancestors have shown you many times
that you are blessed.
Choose faith over doubt.

12
MAY

Learn to be okay with temporary.
Because you yourself do not live forever.

And what a great life you can live
in that limited amount of time.

13
MAY

Anger is a beautiful emotion that allows us
to remember our self-worth.
Never fear your anger.

14
MAY

Once you start loving yourself a little differently,
the people who you choose to love
will be different too.

15
MAY

Love doesn't just happen.
Love is a deliberate choice.
To love someone means to choose them,
every single time.

Love by itself exists in spaces
of mutual decision, appreciation, and care.
Love is always a choice.

16

MAY

I pray that you become comfortable
with healthy love.

17
MAY

When someone leaves,
remember that they do not take
all the love in this world with them.

Rest your heart.
There is so much more love
for you to experience.

18
MAY

You have experienced a lot of weighed-down love.
Your ancestors will make sure that you fly
with the next one.

19
MAY

Learn to not feel suspicious when peace arrives.
Your ancestors give you calmness without tricks.
It's okay—receive it.

20
MAY

You should be proud of yourself.
You chose to live a new life where your needs
no longer come last.
It was no easy feat, and it took courage.
Be proud.

21
MAY

May you never be overwhelmed
by what you asked for.
May you handle your blessings
with tact and strategy.

22
MAY

You are becoming the ocean
after many months of being rain.

In time, grief will bless you with the new beginnings
you never thought were possible.

23
MAY

Pray like your words can shift reality.
Like the Creator is listening.
Like your words can turn anything into gold,
because they can.

24
MAY

Our body is so connected to our emotional state.
Today, practice good posture.

When you shrink into yourself with a curved back,
you are also shrinking your esteem and confidence.

25

MAY

Who you were is not the same person
you will become.
Forgive yourself for your past.
And peacefully welcome change.

26
MAY

When you ask your ancestors
to remove connections that aren't beneficial,
be prepared for who they decide to move.

27
MAY

It's okay to mourn your old life.
This new chapter will soothe your spirit.
You are experiencing the birthing pains
of a new beginning.

28
MAY

Stagnancy also occurs when you ask for too little.
Think bigger.
The universe is too large for you to believe
you're deserving of small blessings.

29
MAY

Hyper-independence kills.
It's okay to ask for help.
And you deserve to receive help
when it's offered to you.

30
MAY

There are people in this world who will show you
pure kindness, love, and respect.
Wait for them.

31
MAY

Trust the process.
Even if the process is taking a lot longer
than what you expected.

June

1

JUNE

Pray for the discernment needed
to differentiate friends from opportunists.

2

JUNE

You are coming into so much good.
So much more love, so much more joy.
It's safe to let the good in.

3

JUNE

You are transforming.
Take some time for yourself today.

Shut the world out and let all of yourself in.

4

JUNE

You have given love your entire life;
it's now your turn to receive.
It's okay to be loved—it's human.

5

JUNE

You've been craving a particular kind of love
within your relationships that you've never
seen before, a love that you know exists.
Don't abandon yourself by settling.
Curate your community.

6

JUNE

Healing becomes less overwhelming
when you focus on one thing at a time.
Take breaks from self-improvement
to simply experience life.

7

JUNE

Try not to be too concerned about gossip.
Instead, keep your character righteous.
The words they use to slander
will only beautify you in the end.

When your hands are clean and your heart is pure,
the fingers that others use to point
will only reflect themselves.
Mind your own character,
not the actions of others.

8

JUNE

Your suffering did not go unnoticed.
Despite it, you will rise.
You will tower over all the things
that wanted to destroy you.
You will not only live; you will flourish.

9

JUNE

When your ancestors bless you,
they are not doing you a favor.
They are giving you what's rightfully yours.
The blessings you have around you
are not by luck or coincidence;
they were fated.

10

JUNE

See life through.
Let life show you just how good it can get.
I promise it will be better
than you could ever imagine.

11

JUNE

It'll be easier on your spirit
if you live in harmony with your shadow,
rather than trying to be all light.
You cannot eat a part of yourself
and still expect to feel full.

We are all dualistic.
Coexist with yourself.

12

JUNE

Your ancestors are currently watching your actions
to see if you truly want a peaceful life
or if you are just saying that.

It's time to swallow your pride
and see how you contribute to your own chaos.
When you finally see it,
take the opportunity to choose differently.

13
JUNE

Anxiety can creep up when we take shallow breaths.
Your breath is what grounds you to Earth.
Take the time to breathe deeply today.

You are safe in your body.

14

JUNE

The road to what you have asked for is now open.
All you have to do is walk the path.
Go confidently.

15

JUNE

There is nothing you can do
to be enough for someone who doesn't like you.
Don't take it personally.
Instead, focus on the love
that you don't have to question.

16
JUNE

Taking care of yourself
makes your manifestations stronger.

Eat well.
Have a sleep schedule.
Breathe deeply.
Stretch.

Your physical and spiritual body will thank you.

17

JUNE

Affirm:

I am deserving of a gentle life
surrounded by beautiful things.

18

JUNE

Free up some space so your ancestors
can bless you this weekend.
Take time to release yourself of old items in your
home and any draining connections around you.
Refresh your altar and be open to the signs.

Make some room for your new life.

19

JUNE

Don't abandon your own needs
by trying to always be so understanding of others.
Being understanding is an amazing trait of empathy.
But be mindful of how many times you allow people
to let you down because you understand.

It's okay to advocate for your needs and desires.
It's okay to tell them when it hurts.

20
JUNE

Joy should be something you consistently
give yourself and not just for special occasions.
Live more often.

21

JUNE

You don't need to give out the title of friend
to everyone who is kind to you.

Kindness is basic human decency.
Be more selective.
Go a bit deeper.

22

JUNE

You're not too broken for love.
Regardless of what you went through
or who you had to become,
you still deserve love.
Right now, as you are.

23

JUNE

You don't need a lot of friends.
You just need the right ones.

Choose quality connections.

24

JUNE

There's no need to look so hard for love.
You are love, just as you are.

25

JUNE

When love arrives,
I pray that you let it in.
I pray that you let it show you things
about yourself.

26
JUNE

Give your shoulders some rest
and release the weight.

Be light like a feather
and allow the burdens to finally roll off.

27

JUNE

You are not an octopus;
there's no need to try to juggle eight things at once.
Please ask for help.
Please receive help when it is given to you.

28

JUNE

You won't lose anything if you choose yourself.
Actually, you will gain so much more.

29

JUNE

The greatest blessing our ancestors give us
is the ability to just be.
To exist.
That is enough.

30

JUNE

Be stubborn about what you want for yourself.
The ancestors favor those
who do not give up so easily.

July

1

JULY

The past has passed.
Constantly telling yourself
how you "should have" done something
is the easiest way to create self-resentment.
You can let it go now.
Rest.

2

JULY

It's going to be okay.
Actually, it's going to be even better than that.
It's going to be more than you could ever dream.

3

JULY

Peace of mind will soon come to you.
And when it arrives,
make sure that you keep it with you.

4

JULY

Affirm:

I give thanks to the unseen forces protecting me
against unforeseen disasters.

5
JULY

Affirm:

I forgive myself for all the times I settled
for the things I didn't want but thought I needed.
I have grown since then.

6

JULY

Trying to manipulate an outcome by controlling
others is the easiest way to become empty.
You are responsible for you.
Knowing this will keep you full.

7

JULY

From now on,
you will no longer know sorrow
more than you know bliss.
Peace will be your new life.

8
JULY

Let the universe take things away in peace.
Breathe.
Not everything has to be a fight.

9

JULY

Relax.
Your success is already owed to you.
All you need to do is show up.

10

JULY

Bit by bit, step-by-step.
The small blessings you notice on your path
lead you to a greater one.
Enjoy the way your legacy is unfolding.

11

JULY

When someone misunderstands you,
it's not an invitation to change your mind.
Stand your ground unapologetically.

It's okay to be misunderstood.
Stand by what you believe.

12

JULY

Become bigger than your ancestors.
It's in your blood to reach further
than they ever could.
It's within your blood to succeed
the generations before you.
Where they couldn't touch, you will surpass.
It's destiny.
Expand.

13

JULY

At peace is the soul that tells others
how it really feels.
At peace is the soul that advocates for itself.

14
JULY

Forgive yourself for all the times you
auditioned for love,
convinced for love,
manipulated for love,
only for it to not stay.
Forgive yourself and proudly change.
Because you deserve a love that stays.

15

JULY

Anger gives us passion.
It signals to us when a boundary has been crossed.
But when there isn't a safe channel for it,
it threatens to swallow you whole.

16
JULY

You can't force someone to accept your love.
Keep it for yourself instead.

17

JULY

The universe speaks to you
because you were born within her.
She lives inside of you.
You are a child of the stars.
And a good mother does not
abandon her children.
She just simply waits for the right time
to intervene.

18
JULY

Your joy is more important than your productivity.

19
JULY

Your ancestors are always hearing you.
Be wise about what you affirm.

20
JULY

Today, if you get the work
you've been putting off done, your ancestors
will reward you with a sweet blessing.
Choose accountability over procrastination.

21
JULY

When you play small, your ancestors will deliver
even smaller blessings to show that you
can have more than what you think you deserve.
The small blessings on your journey
serve the purpose of triggering you
to rethink your capabilities.
If you want bigger blessings,
you cannot be afraid of living a bigger life.

22
JULY

Betrayal will often occur
when you claim everyone as your friend.
Don't make the fatal mistake of confusing
associates or acquaintances for your real friends.

23

JULY

Your love never goes to waste,
even if others put it to the wayside.
Your love is energy.
The universe sees the love you give
and doubles it.
It never goes to waste.

24

JULY

When we rest, we bring in the peace
that is our birthright.
Even when we rest, we will see abundance.
Even when we rest, we will see
all-encompassing blessings.

25

JULY

Just because you're on this healing journey
doesn't mean there won't be bad days.
This journey just gives you the tools
to better navigate these seasons of rain.
Don't give up on yourself.

26

JULY

You look like no other.
You have goals like no other.
You were created as you are for a reason.

You possess the most god-given wisdom
when you are simply being yourself.
Doing what you like, being who you are.
Let that carry you.

27

JULY

You have always been
a kind and considerate person.
That's why the Creator
will make things right for you.

28

JULY

You took care of everybody else;
now it's time to take care of yourself.
You'll lose yourself completely
if you keep making your needs second.
Today, choose yourself.

29

JULY

You spent most of your life
afraid of being too much.
Dare to take the space needed
to breathe comfortably.

30

JULY

This next season of your life will connect you
to the people who will love to help you.
Watch how easy your world will be
when you ask for your help.

31

JULY

Ancestors can't move through your life
if you don't relax your grip.
Surrender the need to control.
Sometimes you don't need to know everything
to move forward.

August

1

AUGUST

The friendships you're forming
are the ones you prayed for.
It's time to build your community.
Helpful people can only be helpful
if you let them.
So, let them.

2

AUGUST

The redirection was strategic.
Go on a different adventure.
Ancestors have the habit of removing you—
by force—from a tree that you should not be climbing.
And it will feel like a loss.
Even in grief, you must trust them
and choose a different path.

3

AUGUST

In this next chapter of your life,
you will live very well.
Strive to do all the things that make you feel
the most alive.

4

AUGUST

You deserve a full, wholehearted love.
A whole love, because you are already whole.

5

AUGUST

Every part of you is worthy.
Even the parts you don't like so much.
You have always been worthy of love.

6

AUGUST

You must enjoy your life
while you're still living it.

Peace is more important than you think.

7

AUGUST

You will get lost many times as you experience life.
Know that you will return home each time.
Celebrate the moments when you remember
who you are.

Ancestors will keep the light on and the food warm
as you find your way back.

8

AUGUST

This newfound comfort and peace
you're stepping into is yours to keep.
Keep it.

9

AUGUST

If you find a creative hobby that's just for you
to enjoy without the pressure to share,
you'll have a key to peace for yourself this year.

10

AUGUST

We're determined to only allow
the versions of love we're comfortable with.
Sometimes we ignore the love we're given
because it doesn't appear the way we're used to.

May you be comfortable with healthy,
honest love.

11
AUGUST

You can't really say that you'll only love
if you won't get hurt again.
To love is to be vulnerable.
To love is to risk.
Trying to avoid heartbreak
will keep your heart closed forever.

When you open yourself up to someone,
you also open yourself to having the sheet ripped
from underneath you at any time.

It can be terrifying to love.
But you must choose to do it anyway,
despite it all.

12
AUGUST

Choose to no longer be an empty body.
Your bones were not created
to hold the sadness of others.

You are not a host, nor a coffin
for people to bury themselves into.
Live.

13

AUGUST

Anger arrives when something
has disrespected your spirit.
It's a powerful emotion,
and when used constructively,
it can create new changes in your life.

14
AUGUST

Arguments are bound to happen.
Pick the ones that are worth fighting for
and leave the rest.

15

AUGUST

What you speak over yourself in the mornings
becomes your destiny.
Speak words of victory, action, faith,
and all good things so your life
can become good too.

16

AUGUST

Sometimes chaos happens for you
to receive wisdom on how to avoid it next time.
Rest your mind.
Everything is taken care of.

17

AUGUST

Isn't it strange that we have to affirm to ourselves
that we are worthy of things such as
kindness, respect, and love,
as if those things are not already our birthright?

Hold on to your birthright.
Know that you don't need to explain why you are
deserving of these things to anyone.

18

AUGUST

It's beautiful how you find new parts of yourself
to love each day.
The amount of love you can pour into yourself
is truly endless.

19

AUGUST

Self-forgiveness is the first crucial step to self-love.
You cannot say you love yourself
when your inner child doesn't trust you.

20

AUGUST

Moisturize yourself with things that smell good.
Wear the clothes that you enjoy.
Take care of yourself.

Make yourself feel like love.
Because you have been love, this entire time.

21

AUGUST

Desiring a romantic partner
doesn't mean you are desperate.
It's okay that you want to spend your life
with somebody else.

Just don't lose yourself by chasing
the wrong ones.

22

AUGUST

Being too nice will always inevitably trap you.
Being too nice is a replica of people-pleasing.
Being so nice that you cross your own
boundaries is not niceness.
It's self-inflicted cruelty on your own spirit.
It's self-abandonment.

Create boundaries and stick to them.
Even if others give you a hard time,
respect yourself and your spirit.

23

AUGUST

There's a lot of deep pain within you
that you don't tell anyone about.
I pray you one day have the courage
to talk about those feelings
and be properly held.

24

AUGUST

Today, you deserve ease.
May this day be gentle on your spirit.

25

AUGUST

As you started to rise in your power,
did people around you begin acting strange?

That's because they only liked you
when they thought you were beneath them.

No matter.
Keep rising.

26

AUGUST

Do not let humility be a scapegoat
for your insecurity.
It's okay to be powerful.

27

AUGUST

Having self-compassion is learning
to not feel guilty when you're exhausted.
It's okay to rest.

28

AUGUST

It's okay to change.
Do not let anyone shame you for it.

We go through experiences that change us
because we don't live this life to remain the same.

Those that shame you for changing
see the way that you can adapt and flow,
while they stay stuck and unmoving.

29

AUGUST

You are leaving darkness and entering the light.
You will now know a life that is filled
with compassion and not suffering.

30

AUGUST

You don't need to have all the answers today.

Or even tomorrow.

Take your time with your growth.

31

AUGUST

It's time to be brave and face the wound
you have been ignoring.
Don't bleed out by trying to keep it all inside.
It's brave to acknowledge the pain.
It's brave to acknowledge that you're not okay.
It's brave to ask for help.
It's brave to heal.

September

1

SEPTEMBER

The world is waiting for you.
And all you have to do is believe in yourself.
The success you're worthy of will be yours
when you decide you're deserving of it.

When you put yourself out there,
you'll be pleasantly surprised by how success
will fall from the sky.

2

SEPTEMBER

You will grow right in front of those
who look down upon you.
And your growth will be massive.

3

SEPTEMBER

It'll come to a point where
you'll have to choose which comes first:
others' opinions of you
or the way you feel about yourself.

The latter will always win in the end.

4

SEPTEMBER

Don't be so caught up in looking for red flags
that you accidentally create them.

5

SEPTEMBER

We're all in this world trying our best.
Many of us are still enduring wars within our bodies.
Let's extend more compassion today.
To ourselves, and outward to others.

6

SEPTEMBER

May today give you victory
over everything that is troubling your mind.
May you rise above it.

7

SEPTEMBER

You are so loved.

Really.

Just in case you haven't heard that today.

8

SEPTEMBER

Remember you are allowed to log out
of social media to take care of yourself.

Be mindful of what you consume today.
Don't let others stress you out.

9

SEPTEMBER

If you're feeling anxious,
it's because you forget to breathe.
Slow down and take a nice inhale.

10

SEPTEMBER

You are in the in-between spot of going and coming,
finding and losing, death and rebirth.
Give yourself grace.

11

SEPTEMBER

Isn't it strange how love and heartbreak
can coexist in the same body?
We are beautiful in our complexity.

12
SEPTEMBER

You still have so much more love to experience.
Be patient.

13

SEPTEMBER

Don't treat your ancestors
like a transactional relationship.
Treat them for what they are—your family.
Ancestral veneration and remembrance
is not about being perfect.
Do not isolate yourself from your people
in times of sorrow.
Your ancestors know you very well.
Show up to them as you are.

14
SEPTEMBER

Other people's inability to return your affection
does not make you any less worthy of love.
Be grateful that you gave.
Be grateful that you opened a part of yourself.

Your ancestors will always take care of you.

15

SEPTEMBER

Life has not forgotten you.
You are deserving of the love you see
being given around you.

That love will soon find you.

16

SEPTEMBER

Affirm:

I forgive myself for enduring loveless love
and believing that's what I deserved.

17

SEPTEMBER

Sometimes people have good intentions.
May you never mistake a genuine friend
for an enemy.

18

SEPTEMBER

Your healing will open gateways
for future descendants and ancestral bodies
to finally be free of heavy generational weight.
Take your time.

19

SEPTEMBER

You don't need to go through hardship to be worthy.
Suffering is not a prerequisite to being blessed.

20

SEPTEMBER

Accepting yourself unconditionally
will give you the freedom you've been looking for.
Some days you may not really like yourself.

To give yourself enough patience
to accept yourself as you are is true healing.

21

SEPTEMBER

Have compassion with the parts of yourself
you deem to be "unlovable."
Those parts are still you.
And they're deserving of gentleness.

Release the need to bully the parts of you
that others rejected.

22

SEPTEMBER

You are still worthy.
Even when you rest,
even when you take your time.

23

SEPTEMBER

You're exhausted because you're fighting change.
Surrender.
And let change come.

24

SEPTEMBER

No one on this earth will ever see you
as you see yourself.

That's why it's so important
to individually validate yourself.

25

SEPTEMBER

You live the best way you can
in a world that attempts to destroy you.
You should give yourself more credit.

26

SEPTEMBER

The Creator already sees you.
You don't need to prove anything to anyone else.

27

SEPTEMBER

Many avoid conflict because they fear
drifting apart from their connections.
What is forgotten is that good conflict resolution
only brings you closer.

It creates mutual vulnerability,
and this brings openness between individuals.
Let's get fluent in the art of relationship repair.

28

SEPTEMBER

Be mindful of binding yourself to self-guilt.
You don't need to be ashamed
of being who you are.

29

SEPTEMBER

Today will be an easy day if you let it be.
Try not to spiral in your thoughts.
Not everything that you think is true.

30

SEPTEMBER

Affirm:

I release the need to doubt my blessings.
Today I choose faith over fear.

October

1

OCTOBER

May your day, week, month
be as beautiful as you are.
As lovely as you are.
As kind as you are.

2

OCTOBER

Try to keep your peace, your laughter,
and your joy today.
No matter what attempts
to throw you off your center.

3

OCTOBER

Do the things you absolutely love today.

Yes, you.

Prioritize your happiness.

4

OCTOBER

May you never stop being kind.
Even when you experience situations
that make you want to change
that part of yourself.

5

OCTOBER

You will shift many times.
You will release many things you thought
you'd hold on to forever.
May you accept every version of yourself.

6

OCTOBER

May you have a long life so you can properly enjoy
all the blessings this world has to offer.

7

OCTOBER

May you realize that there are people
with good intentions.
Sometimes history doesn't have to repeat itself.

8

OCTOBER

Your prayers will reach heaven today.
What do you really want?
Ask, and be open to miracles.

9

OCTOBER

I pray that the universe
gives you an uncomplicated love.
A love that is already open, honest,
and figured out.

10

OCTOBER

Affirm:

I forgive myself for every moment of doubt
that delayed what was rightfully mine.

11

OCTOBER

Rebirth is physically straining on the body.

You must nourish yourself and stay hydrated
so you have the strength to carry yourself
into this new life.

12

OCTOBER

The same lesson will appear in different forms
until you learn to choose differently.

To have a prosperous future,
you must remember your past experiences
and intentionally walk a different road.

The universe blesses those
who choose to break their cycles.

13

OCTOBER

The universe needs you.
This is the season of wins
and stepping into yourself.

14

OCTOBER

If you don't fight for yourself,
this world will do a good job
of swallowing you up.

Take your peace by force.

15

OCTOBER

The idea in your head won't leave you
until you finally bring it to life.
Your ancestors are patiently watching;
it's time to begin.

16

OCTOBER

The universe remembers your suffering.
This is why compassion is owed to you.

You are deserving of receiving a life
that is filled with compassion, not suffering.

17

OCTOBER

The universe didn't create you with doubt.
It birthed you with full awareness
of your capabilities.

Believe in yourself,
just like how the stars believe in you.

18

OCTOBER

Affirm:

Ancestors, please give me a love
that is sweet as honey and bright like the sun.

Let it be a love that I don't need to heal from.

19

OCTOBER

Affirm:

I am patient with myself
and the life I want to create.

20

OCTOBER

Affirm:

I am already whole,
so I only accept whole things.

Half love and half intentions
will never fill me.

21

OCTOBER

Take a look around you.
You're coming into everything
you dreamed about.

Rejoice.

22

OCTOBER

When opportunities cross your path
and you're hesitant to accept them,
remember that you have always been qualified.
It's time to let go of the stories of yourself that were
told by those who didn't want to see you succeed.

You have always been deserving of an abundant life.
You have always been worthy.

23

OCTOBER

There will be people you'll meet
who want to love you, be around you,
and support you just because of your heart.

Believe them.

24

OCTOBER

You deserve peace in your life,
not just low stress.
There's a difference.

25

OCTOBER

The day will soon arrive
when your thoughts won't swallow you whole.
Your mind will not stay an abyss forever.
You will find the stillness you're looking for.
Trust.

26

OCTOBER

They can love you.
Or not.
Either way,
you'll still be okay in the end.

27

OCTOBER

Be mindful of rushing to fix sadness.
Give sadness the space in your body to breathe,
to exist, without trying to morph it
into a new emotion.

28

OCTOBER

Impatient parenting is one reason why many people
struggle with issues like conflict resolution,
people-pleasing, an overly critical inner voice,
and hyper-independence.

Reparent yourself by practicing patience.

29

OCTOBER

It's okay to be wrong, but it's important
to be accountable when you are corrected.
Humility matters.

30

OCTOBER

Maybe the goal shouldn't be
constant joy or happiness, but peace.
A cool neutral.

To experience life with a balanced center,
no matter what.

31

OCTOBER

Other people's dislike of you should not be
the reason for you to dislike yourself.

You're the one in your body, after all.

November

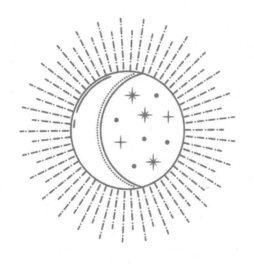

1

NOVEMBER

It's time to see the intentions of others clearly.
Don't deceive yourself by believing everyone
is as kindhearted as you are.

2

NOVEMBER

Acknowledge all the emotions
you're currently suppressing.
Stop trying to think your way
through your feelings.
Feel them.

Today is the day to rebalance yourself.

3

NOVEMBER

Embrace change.
Everything around you changes constantly.
All that's left is for you to change too.

4

NOVEMBER

I pray that the worries of yesterday
will not follow you into the beginning of today.

5

NOVEMBER

You're too blessed for the other shoe to drop.
This is your new life, get used to ease.

6

NOVEMBER

This is the month of collaboration and connection.
Two heads are better than one.
Partnerships can happen in unexpected places,
so keep your mind and heart open.

7

NOVEMBER

The world depends on your own vision.
Your voice will always find the ones who need it.

The universe blesses those
who can just be themselves.

8

NOVEMBER

If your ancestors were really telling you no,
you wouldn't be getting so close to your goal.
Push through the resistance.
You'll be glad you did.

9

NOVEMBER

A lucky streak is happening for you.
But it's not because of luck—
it's because of divine intervention.

10

NOVEMBER

It's not always about you.
Once you understand this,
you'll start to feel a little freer in your spirit.

11

NOVEMBER

Trying to be liked by everybody will make you say and do things you don't really resonate with. Good character lies in being yourself.

12

NOVEMBER

It's time to listen to your body.

If you need to cry, cry.
If you need to sleep, sleep.
If you need to eat, eat.

It's okay to give yourself what you need.

13

NOVEMBER

Be mindful of too much humility to the point
where you don't even acknowledge your own success.
Celebrate.
You deserve it.

14

NOVEMBER

Do not let anyone take the peace
that you have worked so hard to create.
Protect this new life of tranquility
that you have built for yourself.

15

NOVEMBER

Today, life will get better.
Enjoy how easy things will start to be for you.

You don't always have to work harder
to get what you want.

16

NOVEMBER

Anxiety can happen
when you try to do things quickly.
Mind your breath.
Take it slow and take your time.

17

NOVEMBER

Don't get distracted.
You are very close to bringing in
everything you asked for.

Stay focused.

18

NOVEMBER

Release the fear of being too much.
You come from your ancestors,
who were bigger than life.
Make them proud.

19

NOVEMBER

Stop silently wanting things.
All you have to do is ask.
There are people who want to help you,
but they do not know what you need.
Open your mouth
and let them hear your truth.

20

NOVEMBER

The way you take care of yourself
is the way your ancestors will take care of you.
It's time to drench yourself in love.

21

NOVEMBER

Whatever has been lost
will be returned to you in new forms.
This way, you will always feel full,
never empty.

22

NOVEMBER

Sit up straight.
In this next level of your life,
you are not allowed to play small.

23

NOVEMBER

An opening for the impossible
to become a reality has appeared.
The gate is open for you.
Walk through it.

24

NOVEMBER

Social media cannot be your only hobby.
It may lead to you feeling drained and uninspired.
Look up.

25

NOVEMBER

Stop praying for sweet connections
while still accepting poison.
Your actions must match your desires.

You deserve more.

26

NOVEMBER

Go back to yourself.
Release the burdens of others
that you accidentally camouflaged as your own.

Recreate yourself and watch how miracles
materialize out of thin air.

27

NOVEMBER

This next season is about readjusting your focus.
Take your energy back and invest in your legacy.

Invest in a routine that feels good.
Invest your time with the people
that make you feel safe.
Invest in yourself.

Your legacy is the peace you create.

28

NOVEMBER

Giving is not the problem.
Over-giving is.

Be mindful of leaving others so full
that you yourself become empty.
Just like how good a delicious meal is,
you can still eat too much and end up
not taking the time to truly enjoy it.

Don't let people mindlessly consume you.
You're more precious than that.

29

NOVEMBER

If you fight for everyone to stay in your life,
when do you have the time to fight for yourself?
Accept that like the seasons,
people come and people go.

30

NOVEMBER

Wishing you good luck
on your journey back to yourself.
May the blessings you find on your way
make the path not feel in vain.

December

1

DECEMBER

Love grows where joy lives.
Where fun and play exists.
Don't take it so seriously.

2

DECEMBER

You carry yourself wherever you go.
Make sure you're a safe place for you to be
and thrive in perfect harmony.

3

DECEMBER

Your ancestors will make sure
that any obstacles blocking your path this month
will be destroyed and overcome.

4

DECEMBER

When you start speaking detailed prayers,
you'll see how the universe and your ancestors
will bend reality to give you what you asked for.

5

DECEMBER

Imagination and intuition go together.
Hold on to your creativity so the universe
can hold on to you.

6

DECEMBER

Your ancestors can truly bless you with so much.

But if you believe you don't deserve it,
it will always fall short.

7

DECEMBER

Practice gratitude more often.
There is much to be thankful for,
even when it doesn't seem like it.
Remember gratitude is not just
for big blessings or accomplishments.
You can be grateful for breath,
you can be thankful for life.

8

DECEMBER

You see how life became quieter when the universe
took away certain people from you?
Enjoy how this peace feels.

9

DECEMBER

The universe will not give you what you want
if what you want hurts you in the end.

Delays and redirection are ancestral protection.

10

DECEMBER

The universe answers your need.
Sometimes the things you want
are not always the things you need.
Pray for discernment.

11

DECEMBER

What accomplishment did you have this year
that you brushed off?
Take some time to celebrate
before you reach this year's end.
Give yourself proper credit.
Feel your accomplishments in your chest.

12

DECEMBER

Affirm:

I deserve to be surrounded by those
who nurture the potential they see in me,
rather than those who attempt to destroy it.

13

DECEMBER

Once you overcome your fear of being seen
for who you truly are,
you'll unlock new types of blessings.

14

DECEMBER

Opportunity finally arrives in loads.
All you've got to do is say yes.

For the past few weeks,
you have been a good farmer.
This month you'll reap your abundance.
But it'll be larger than you expected.
It's for you.

Say yes when it comes.

15

DECEMBER

When you extend a hand to help someone
or pay it forward, you'll be creating a more
successful life for yourself in the end.

16

DECEMBER

This year held a lot of grief.
That's okay.
May today be at least sweet on you.

17

DECEMBER

Whenever you feel disconnected
from your ancestors, take that
as an opportunity go deeper into yourself.
You are being given a chance to trust yourself
and the particular wisdom that only
your spirit can tap into.

18

DECEMBER

Your ancestors want to give you longevity,
but you must possess the energy to sustain it first.
So, rest and get your spirit together.

19

DECEMBER

This next stage of your life
will require you to be perceived.
And to be perceived wrongly.

Where your journey is taking you
will require you to be okay with it.

20

DECEMBER

You already learned the lesson.
Now it's time to forgive yourself.
Enjoy the rest of your life
with newfound wisdom.

21

DECEMBER

Your smile heals.
Not just for others, but for yourself as well.
Keep it on you.

22

DECEMBER

I pray that your growth be so tall that the evil sent
from your enemies will not be able to touch you.

I pray that your enemies get arrogant
and try to reach for you anyway—
only for their evil to fall back to them.

23

DECEMBER

Affirm:

I forgive myself for all the times I held my tongue.
For all the times I edited my speech for others.
Now, I speak my truth.

24

DECEMBER

You worked so hard for this moment.
Your new life is finally beginning
and you deserve all of it.
Step into yourself.

25

DECEMBER

What you write about becomes your life.
Write beyond yourself.
Write yourself into new realities,
new worlds where you're victorious.
Then sit back and watch as your environment shifts
to hold everything you wrote into existence.

26

DECEMBER

Your dreams are where your spirit can fly
without dying.
Heed the messages given.

27

DECEMBER

If you cannot fly, you can swim.
Try a different approach and be flexible.
Sometimes you just need to ask for help.

28

DECEMBER

Take more pictures of yourself.
It's not self-centered.
You have features that are unlike anything
this world has ever seen;
embrace them.

29

DECEMBER

Trust in the redirection.
Everything will become clearer in time.
Wait and see.

30

DECEMBER

Pay attention to the ways
you make yourself feel unworthy of love.

31

DECEMBER

Today will be an emotional earthquake
as we shake this year off our bones.
It's okay to acknowledge the burdens
this year caused.

Give your grief to the moon.

Acknowledgments

Thank you to the Hay House team for taking beautiful care of my book, and thank you to my community members for encouraging me to put my words down in ink.

About the Author

Ehime Ora, also known as Ifawole Sangodosu Erinfunto Osunfunmike Adeola, is a Nigerian writer, artist, and priestess of the Ifa & Orisa tradition. Ora is initiated into the societies of Ifa, Sango, Erinle, and Osun and is titled as an Iyanifa and Iyalorisa respectively. Ehime has dedicated her life to becoming one of the many bridges for those searching for ancestral connection, generational healing, and personal alignment with the use of African philosophy and ancestral technology. Through her creations, she facilitates tangible joy and spiritual well-being within her community.

Hay House Titles of Related Interest

THE SHIFT, the movie,
starring Dr. Wayne W. Dyer
(available as an online streaming video)
www.hayhouse.com/the-shift-movie

* * *

AFRICAN GODDESS INITIATION:
Sacred Rituals for Self-Love, Prosperity and Joy,
by Abiola Abrams

CHANGE ENTHUSIASM:
How to Harness the Power of Emotion for Leadership and Success,
by Cassandra Worthy

ANGEL PRAYERS:
Harnessing the Help of Heaven to Create Miracles,
by Kyle Gray

KNOW JUSTICE KNOW PEACE:
A Transformative Journey of Social Justice, Anti-Racism,
and Healing through the Power of the Enneagram,
by Deborah Threadgill Egerton, Ph.D., with Lisi Mohandessi

THE HIGH 5 HABIT:
Take Control of Your Life with One Simple Habit,
by Mel Robbins

All of the above are available at your local bookstore
or may be ordered by visiting:

Hay House USA: www.hayhouse.com®
Hay House Australia: www.hayhouse.com.au
Hay House UK: www.hayhouse.co.uk
Hay House India: www.hayhouse.co.in

We hope you enjoyed this Hay House book. If you'd like to receive our online catalog featuring additional information on Hay House books and products, or if you'd like to find out more about the Hay Foundation, please contact:

Hay House, Inc., P.O. Box 5100, Carlsbad, CA 92018-5100
(760) 431-7695 or (800) 654-5126
(760) 431-6948 (fax) or (800) 650-5115 (fax)
www.hayhouse.com® • www.hayfoundation.org

———

Published in Australia by: Hay House Australia Pty. Ltd.,
18/36 Ralph St., Alexandria NSW 2015
Phone: 612-9669-4299 • *Fax:* 612-9669-4144
www.hayhouse.com.au

Published in the United Kingdom by: Hay House UK, Ltd.,
The Sixth Floor, Watson House, 54 Baker Street, London W1U 7BU
Phone: +44 (0)20 3927 7290 • *Fax:* +44 (0)20 3927 7291
www.hayhouse.co.uk

Published in India by: Hay House Publishers India,
Muskaan Complex, Plot No. 3, B-2, Vasant Kunj, New Delhi 110 070
Phone: 91-11-4176-1620 • *Fax:* 91-11-4176-1630
www.hayhouse.co.in

———

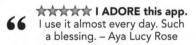